I Got This!

30-Day Tips for Black Women with Anxiety or Depression

Latoya Johnson-Foster, MA, LPC

This book contains the opinions of the author and how she managed her symptoms of anxiety and depression. This book is not intended to replace the work of a mental health professional. For severe cases, please seek professional help.

18.5% of U.S. Adults experience mental illness with a given year and African Americans are 20% more likely to experience serious mental health problems (Mental Health by the Numbers, n.d.).

Depression does not occur alone and has a high co-occurrence rate with anxiety and substance use disorders (Depression Hotline Number, n.d.).

Studies suggest that blacks with anxiety experience the disorder for longer periods of time than their white counterparts (Neal-Barnett, Stadulis, Murray, Payne, Thomas, and Salley, 2011).

African American women were more likely to report feeling of sadness, hopelessness, and worthlessness than European American women (Watson and Hunter, 2015).

To my black women suffering silently, find comfort in knowing that you don't have to fight this battle alone, so you can begin seeking professional help and help from your support system.

Day 1

Good morning beautiful. You've got this!

Sometimes it's hard to start the day after a restless night, but give yourself a pep talk to get going.

Tip: Meditate for five minutes to clear your mind. Try doing a deep breathing technique, slowly inhale through your nose and exhale out of your mouth.

Daily Reflection

Day 2

Smile until you feel better. Laugh like there is no tomorrow!

At times, a smile can make you feel better. A smile is like a mind trick that can alter your mood. If you want to feel better, smile until it becomes your reality.

Tip: Maintain a positive attitude and put your stress into perspective by evaluating the problem you're thinking about. Will it matter a day from now? A week? A month? If not, then free your mind from the problem.

Daily Reflection

Day 3

Wake up and slay. Today is going to be a great day!

It's important to claim a good and victorious day as soon as your feet hit the floor! Sometimes, the difference between a good and bad day is your attitude. Remember, you determine the outcome of your day!

Tip: Take a few minutes to look in the mirror and speak one to three positive affirmations to yourself.

Daily Reflection

Day 4

Think positive. Feel positive. Be positive!

It's as simple as that. If you want to feel better, you must change your thoughts to improve your mood. Don't let negativity or self-doubt in!

Tip: Be mindful of what you allow to penetrate your ears and mind. Listen to uplifting music or watch something inspirational to help make that possible.

Daily Reflection

Day 5

Put on the cute outfit that's been on your mind. Do your make-up and enjoy your day! Don't think about what needs to be done tomorrow or the next day. Simply focus on today!

When you are dealing with anxiety, you tend to overthink a lot of things. Today, don't allow that to happen.

Tip: If you find yourself overthinking, do a technique called "thought stopping." It's as simple as consciously saying "Stop!" Interrupt those racing thoughts by replacing it with positive ones.

Daily Reflection

Day 6

The past has no place in your present. Don't worry yourself about things you can't change.

Focusing on the past doesn't allow you to enjoy the present moment, because you think about things you can't change. Accept what is and move on.

Tip: Allow yourself to be completely and totally in the moment. A technique you can use is grounding which requires that you focus on something in your surroundings that you can see, feel, hear, or smell. Try doing this technique for five minutes until you are present again.

Daily Reflection

_____
_____
_____
_____
_____
_____
_____
_____
_____
_____
_____
_____
_____
_____
_____
_____
_____
_____
_____
_____

Day 7

Today don't doubt yourself. Go with the flow!

Anxiety causes you to overthink, worry, and even fear things that haven't happened. Have confidence in your decision making today.

Tip: Self-doubt is your worst enemy. Instead of thinking the worst, try thinking of the best possible outcome only.

Daily Reflection

Day 8

You are stronger than you know for holding everything together the way that you do.

Today, release that feeling of having to be Superwoman and just allow yourself to be human. Ask for help. Admit that you can't handle all things by yourself. Lean on your support system for help.

Tip: Put your Superwoman cape down and reach out to someone for help. Don't assume that people don't want to help you if you haven't asked them too.

Daily Reflection

Day 9

Don't overcommit yourself today by saying yes when you really want to say no.

It's okay to say no sometimes, especially when you have a lot on your plate. Be aware of how much you can handle without overdoing it.

Tip: Learn how to set healthy boundaries. You don't always have to say yes to people.

Daily Reflection

Day 10

Start your day off by saying, "Today will be amazing!"

Celebrate whatever accomplishments you will achieve today by not overlooking the small steps it'll take to make it possible.

Tip: Plan a dinner date with your significant other or close friend to celebrate your accomplishments.

Daily Reflection

Day 11

You are capable of endless possibilities!

Today, make it a point to not let negative thoughts creep in your mind and have you think that you are not good enough. You are more than enough!

Tip: To help with this, try journaling to express your thoughts when you are in need of instant relief.

Daily Reflection

Day 12

Feelings of sadness will not hold you hostage today.

When experiencing depression, getting out of bed, eating food, or even leaving the house can sometimes be hard to do. Take a moment to think about what's triggering your sadness.

Tip: Talk to a therapist, friend, significant other, or a family member about your feelings. Don't feel like you're all alone with no help.

Daily Reflection

Day 13

Look in the mirror and say, "I am able. I am smart. I am worthy of all things great!"

Positive affirmations are beneficial to your mental and emotional wellbeing. Look in the mirror and speak life into yourself.

Tip: Don't get in your own way today. Step aside and be the best possible version of yourself.

Daily Reflection

Day 14

If you woke up feeling like today isn't your day, then push harder and make today your day!

Remember that your thoughts and mood will determine how your day goes. Only you have the power to control that.

Tip: Eat a well-balanced healthy breakfast or listen to some upbeat music to give you energy.

Daily Reflection

Day 15

Don't focus on the future. It takes away from your present.

Instead of focusing on the "what ifs," focus on what is and allow yourself to enjoy this moment.

Tip: You can do a five-minute relaxation technique focusing on deep breathing to disengage your mind from distracting thoughts.

Daily Reflection

Day 16

You are more than enough. Now show the world how bad ass you are!

People may forget how amazing you are, but you shouldn't be one of them.

Tip: Be mindful of how you treat yourself. Accept your flaws, so that you can recognize all the wonderful things you are capable of!

Daily Reflection

Day 17

You have been doing so great lately. Keep going!

Take a moment to reflect on making it past the halfway point of this book. Look at you growing and glowing! If you haven't heard it today then let me say it, "I am proud of you!"

Tip: Take a few moments to self-reflect so you can see how far you've come and where you're heading.

Daily Reflection

Day 18

Make today count by not overthinking and second guessing yourself!

Second guessing yourself is typical when you are dealing with anxiety. However, give yourself some credit. So what if you don't get it right? Life goes on!

Tip: If you find yourself overthinking, use the thought stopping technique on Day 5 of this guide. Replace the irrational thoughts with rational ones.

Daily Reflection

Day 19

Surround yourself with people who love you.

Energy is contagious. Sometimes, surrounding yourself with people who have positive energy can rub off on you. Know that you are not alone, and you need that positive energy from other people.

Tip: Be intentional with who you are around today. Relax and do something fun with the people you love.

Daily Reflection

Day 20

Identify the internal pressures you're dealing with and release them. Ask yourself are they realistic or unrealistic?

Your family and friends are not expecting you to be perfect. Your need to be perfect and without flaw is unhealthy. Be human, make mistakes, forgive yourself, and move on!

Tip: Don't be afraid to let go of those internal pressures placed upon yourself. Get a planner and set realistic goals for you to accomplish.

Daily Reflection

Day 21

Believe in yourself. You are enough! You are beautiful! You are fearfully and wonderfully made!

You were created from the most high and no one can tell you any different, not even yourself.

Tip: Let go of any insecurity you're silently battling. Turn your cants into cans!

Daily Reflection

Day 22

Focus on your triggers today. Write down what happens right before you get in a sad mood or have negative thoughts.

Identifying your triggers is the start of your healing journey. You have to be aware of what's setting you off, so you can begin managing your symptoms.

Tip: Find and print a daily mood chart online, so that you can begin keeping track of your different moods and what's going right before those negative thoughts/feelings happen.

Daily Reflection

Day 23

Focus on the things that make you happy and brings you peace.

Your mental health is important. To be there for your family, you must be mentally well. Maybe today can be a self-care day?

Tip: If you can, go get a massage at the spa. There is an aura of peaceful energy to help relax you while at the spa.

Daily Reflection

Day 24

Don't let feelings of hopelessness get the best of you.

By now it should be a little easier to do a coping technique. Rejoice in the fact that you have made it this far!

Tip: Focus on where you're at today: physically, mentally, emotionally, and spiritually.

Daily Reflection

Day 25

You will get through this day and will be okay.

You've survived so many days that you didn't know you could get through. Today is no different.

Tip: Clap for yourself today. Praise yourself for doing the necessary work to keep you on track.

Daily Reflection

Day 26

Give yourself permission to be human. You don't have to tackle everything by yourself today.

You know that you are strong and can handle most things thrown your way. However, don't be afraid to ask for help when you are struggling.

Tip: People can only help you when they are aware of what's going on. Pick up the phone to call or send a text asking for the help you need.

Daily Reflection

Day 27

Focus on things that are in your control.

Anxiety causes you worry about things that are out of your control. Focus on things that are only within your grasp.

Tip: Control the controllable. Pay close attention to what you can realistically handle.

Daily Reflection

Day 28

Make yourself a priority today.

Take care of those personal things you've been avoiding for a while. Whatever you choose to do, make it all about you!

Tip: Pace yourself today. You don't have to rush to get everything done. Remember that you are the focus.

Daily Reflection

Day 29

Take a moment to thank yourself for the goodness of your personality.

You are not perfect. Nobody is. However, you are a blessing to yourself and others.

Tip: Be mindful of the energy you put into the world today. Be conscious in your thinking and feelings. Try focusing on things in your surroundings that you haven't noticed before.

Daily Reflection

Day 30

Congratulate yourself for spending the last 30 days working on becoming a better you. You are stronger than you think, and this past month has proven that.

Anxiety and depression are two mental illnesses that happens to most people. You must determine how it'll effect your life. You have the power to fight it by learning how to manage your symptoms!

Tip: Don't forget the many coping mechanisms you've learned over the past month. Start this book over if you need too, but whatever you do, don't give up on yourself!

Daily Reflection

Resources

Neal-Barnett, A., Stadulis, R., Murray, M., Payne, M. R., Thomas, A., & Salley, B. B. (2011). Sister circles as a culturally relevant intervention for anxious black women. *Clinical Psychology: Science and Practice, 18(3)*, 266-273.

Watson, N. N., & Hunter, C. D. (2015). Anxiety and depression among African American women: The costs of strength and negative attitudes toward psychological help-seeking. *Cultural Diversity & Ethnic Minority Psychology, 21(4)*, 604-612.

Websites

Depression Hotline Number. www.mentalhelp.net

Mental Health By the Numbers. www.nami.org

Acknowledgements

To my husband, Michael. Thank you for being there for me selflessly and loving me unconditionally during my struggle. I love you to infinity and beyond!

To my daughter, Kyla. You have been such an inspiration to me and giving me the strength I needed to press forward. I love you!

To my mother, Maetean. You don't know how much our daily talks helped make me laugh and forget I was going through. You mean the world to me!

To my family and friends. I thank you all so much for being there for me once I opened myself to you. I appreciate the role all of you play in my life.

About the Author

Latoya Johnson-Foster is a licensed professional counselor with experience providing counseling to teens and adults with anxiety and/or depression. She has a BA in Psychology from Chicago State University and an MA in Marriage and Family Counseling from Governors State University. She has experienced both anxiety and depression firsthand, so she understands how difficult it can be to find ways of coping and managing those symptoms. More information and tips can be found at www.latoyajfoster.com

Made in the USA
Monee, IL
06 May 2022